C902543650

Fact Finders®

TechSafetyTips

SAFE Social Networking

by Heather E. Schwartz

raintree
a Capstone company — publishers for children

Raintree is an imprint of Capstone Global Library Limited, a company incorporated in England and Wales having its registered office at 264 Banbury Road, Oxford, OX2 7DY – Registered company number: 6695582

www.raintree.co.uk
myorders@raintree.co.uk

Jennifer Besel, editor; Sarah Bennett, designer; Laura Manthe, production specialist

ISBN 978 1 4747 2426 5
20 19 18 17 16
10 9 8 7 6 5 4 3 2

British Library Cataloguing in Publication Data
A full catalogue record for this book is available from the British Library.

Acknowledgements
We would like to thank the following for permission to reproduce photographs: Capstone Studio: Karon Dubke, 5, 13; Dreamstime: Outline205, 25; iStockphotos: Jodi Matthews, 9; Shutterstock: Aikaterini Dimopoulou, 18-19, bcdan, 16, Darrin Henry, 5 (inset), ilyaka, 28-29 (silhouettes), iQoncept, 14-15, John T Takai, 24, Jojje, 12, jugulator, 10 (all), justone, 6, Laschon Robert Paul, 20, mast3r, 23, Olha Onishchuk, 27 (all), Piti Tan, 28, venimo, 28, 29 (icons), Vinogradov Illya, 21, vitdesignpv, 17, VLADGRIN, cover (network, icons)
Artistic Effects: Shutterstock: Bennyart, ilyaka, John T Takai, Mikhail, nagib, nrt, SoooInce, vendor, VLADGRIN.

We would like to thank Frank W. Baker, Media Literacy Consultant at Media Literacy Clearinghouse Inc. for his invaluable help in the preparation of this book.

Every effort has been made to contact copyright holders of material reproduced in this book. Any omissions will be rectified in subsequent printings if notice is given to the publisher.

All the internet addresses (URLs) given in this book were valid at the time of going to press. However, due to the dynamic nature of the internet, some addresses may have changed, or sites may have changed or ceased to exist since publication. While the author and publisher regret any inconvenience this may cause readers, no responsibility for any such changes can be accepted by either the author or the publisher.

Made in China

Contents

Your online world 4

Watch out! 10

Fixing it 16

Ways to deal 22

Glossary 30

Read more 31

Website 31

Index 32

Your online world

What do you like best about social networking? Connecting with friends? Writing clever posts? Or maybe posting pictures? Whatever the answer, everything you do while social networking helps form your online **reputation**. Your online reputation tells people who you are and what you're all about. When you take responsibility for what you put online, you control your reputation and your safety.

But there is a part of social networking you can't control. You can't choose how other people use technology. Suppose someone posted a mean message about you. Should you ignore it or write back? You can choose how to react. When making that decision, remember that your reaction will affect your image and safety both online and off.

reputation your worth or character, as judged by other people

Keesha Miller
Today at 4:47pm

OMG!!! Tanya's shirt is so ugly!

Like - Comment 👍 1 💬 12

Talk about it

Throughout this book, you'll find "Talk about it" boxes that set up real-life situations you might run into. Use these boxes as discussion starters at home or at school. Talk about the pros and cons of different actions, and decide how you could stay safe in each situation.

So, what should you do if you read a mean post about yourself?

Follow the rules

One way to protect yourself is to use a
site that's right for you. People of all ages use
social networking sites. Some sites are designed
especially for kids under age 13. They're created
with safety in mind. These sites won't let kids
connect with others who are not close in age.
These sites may also check posts to remove
hurtful comments.

Other social networking sites are meant for users ages 13 and up. While that means fewer **restrictions**, it also means greater risks. When kids use these sites, they're not as protected from **cyberbullies**. Kids could also be contacted by adult strangers.

It can be tempting to create a page on an adult social networking site. But following the rules has benefits. You keep yourself safe. You also prove to trusted adults that you can be responsible online. Your actions will build trust and help you earn more privileges as you get older.

Talk about it

All your friends join a popular social networking site. The rules of the site say users have to be 18 years old to join. But by using a fake birthday, anyone can get in. You don't want to be left out.

What should you do?

restriction rule or limitation

cyberbully person who uses technology to spread mean messages, rumours or threats

Too much information?

If social networking was described in one word, it would be sharing. Users share everything from their relationship statuses to the meals they're eating. But there is such a thing as too much information.

Sharing private information online is never a good idea. Dishonest people could use it to steal your online **identity**. They could even use your private info to apply for credit cards or **loans**, all while pretending to be you!

It's not always easy to know what's public and what's private info. One good clue – public information helps others get to know you. For example, your likes and dislikes are public information.

Private info is information you don't want to share with others. If the information is embarrassing, it's definitely private. If it might allow strangers to contact you in real life, that's private too. It also includes information that can help people get more information about you. For example, you may feel fine telling someone where your parents work. But that information could be used to find out if you're home alone.

identity who you are

loan money borrowed from a bank

WEIGHING THE INFO

Public info includes anything you don't mind telling the whole world. Private info includes things you need to keep to yourself. Before sharing, stop and think about which category the info would fall into.

FIRST NAME

FAVOURITE FOODS

BOOKS YOU'RE READING

FAVOURITE MOVIE

SPORTS YOU PLAY

PET'S NAME

PUBLIC INFO

LAST NAME

PASSWORDS

HOME ADDRESS

E-MAIL ADDRESS

WHERE YOU ARE OR WHERE YOU'RE GOING

NATIONAL INSURANCE NUMBER

PRIVATE INFO

Watch out!

Social networking is a lot of fun. But sometimes people forget to stay aware of their actions. As a responsible user, always remember that what you do online can affect you offline too.

When you're chatting online, it may feel just like talking with people face-to-face. But there are some big differences. For one thing, in real life you can see the people you're dealing with. You can also read their body language, facial expressions and tone of voice. All of these clues improve communication so the right messages come across.

You can't read facial expressions online!

Online communication is trickier. Written messages can be misunderstood. For example, when you post a joke online, a friend might take your words seriously. When this happens in real life, you can clear up the problem right away. But when it happens online, you might not realize how your friend really feels.

Some people use the internet for dishonest purposes. They **pose** as others when they're online. Cyberbullies, for example, may pose as friends. Adult strangers can pretend to be young kids or teenagers. When you're online, you can't tell whether a person is lying. Keeping private information to yourself is great protection from these risks.

Talk about it

You're chatting with a new friend you met through a social networking site. He says he's 12 years old and even sends a picture of himself. But once in a while he uses big words you don't know. You start to wonder if he's really who he says he is.

What do you do?

pose pretend to be someone else

Picture this

Sharing photos is part of the fun of social networking. But it's important to carefully choose which photos you post. Some may give information that shouldn't be shared. Many mobile phones, for example, use **geotagging**. It tells where you were when a photo was taken. If you post a picture while on holiday, you could let strangers know your family isn't home.

Embarrassing photos can also cause trouble. Sometimes they appear when cyberbullies alter them. An altered photo might make it look as though you're behaving badly. That could hurt your online image.

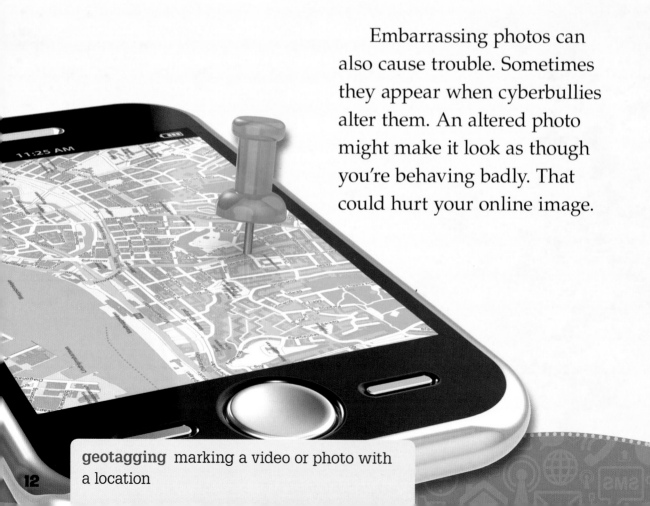

geotagging marking a video or photo with a location

In most cases, you can control the images that are posted on your page. Check with friends before posting their pictures. Make sure they're OK with the images you're sharing. Images you share online should not give away private information or embarrass anyone.

Picture perfect?

Look closely at this picture. It's not the best image to post online, but can you tell why?

1460
CHESTNUT AVE.

Did you find the problems with the picture?
The kid on the left is wearing a shirt that tells what town the kids live in. And the sign in the background shows where the photo was taken. Both of these things are private info. Also, the poor girl spilling food on herself will be embarrassed to have this photo posted all over the web.

Out-of-control apps

You're online and notice a link to an interesting article. The subject is a little embarrassing, but you're alone in your room. Who's going to know what you read? You click on the link and get the scoop. Then you head to your social networking page. That's when you realize the **publication** shared what you read with everyone you know.

How could this happen? It starts with your decision to use apps. Sometimes an app is the only way to read an article a friend wants to share. Using the app may seem harmless. The only problem? These apps post on your social networking site everything you read. And they don't ask permission.

publication book, magazine or newspaper

Over-sharing is certainly a danger with these apps. After all, what you choose to read online may be private information. How can you protect yourself? Don't use the apps unless you can choose what gets shared.

Talk about it

You use your mum's smartphone while you're waiting for the dentist. You click on an article from your friend's social networking site. To view it, though, you have to download an app. You download it, but then it's your turn to get your teeth cleaned. Later that day, you realize your mum doesn't know you downloaded that app.

What do you do?

Fixing it

Everyone makes mistakes. So what do you do when you make an online mess? Sometimes online mistakes can be easily repaired. Suppose you accidentally give out too much information about when and where you're meeting friends. Don't panic. Just change your plans with a few quick phone calls.

The same kind of quick action can solve problems with pictures posted online. See yourself in a bad photo on another person's page? Contact that person or the site administrator. Ask them to remove the image. If the picture's on your own page, take it down yourself.

In other cases, the **consequences** of a social networking mistake could be harsher. Imagine what could happen if you fired off a mean comment about a classmate. You could hurt someone's feelings. You could inspire others to make mean comments too.

It's not easy to backtrack once you've cyberbullied someone. It may help to apologize for what you've said. But the best thing to do is avoid cyberbullying behaviour in the first place. Walk away from your computer if you're angry or upset. Do something else to calm down. When you're ready to return, post something kinder or avoid the topic altogether.

consequence result of an action

The long haul

Right now social networking mistakes may not seem like a big deal. But you need to know that a bad online reputation can cause problems in the future too. Once information is posted online, it's tough to get rid of. You can delete a message or photo from your own site. But it could have been saved and shared by other users. Universities could see these posts and images when you apply. Employers could find them too. As a result, your university application might be rejected. You might not be hired for a job you really want.

Make sure posts reflect the real you.

But don't worry if your online reputation is less than perfect. There are steps you can take to repair it. Take down your old social networking page and create a new one. Make sure everything you post reflects you as you want to be known. You can't control what others say about you online. But you can put positive information out there. This action will make it more difficult for anyone to find negative information about you.

Serious situations

Sometimes you may find yourself talking with a stranger on a social networking site. Be extra careful in this situation. People online could be trying to trick you. Watch for these warning signs.

Online friends SHOULD NOT:

- pressure you to chat privately, either in a private chat room or by instant message, e-mail or phone.

- send messages or photos that make you uncomfortable.

- insist on meeting in real life and try to make you feel guilty or silly for hesitating.

If any red flags pop up, talk to a trusted adult right away. He or she can help you unfriend that person and report him or her to the police if necessary.

Social networking gets much riskier when online friends decide to meet in real life. Sometimes online friends turn out to be adult strangers. They lied in order to trick a child.

Not all online friends turn out to be dangerous. But it's better to be very cautious. If you want to meet an online friend in person, talk to a parent or trusted adult first. Make sure an adult comes with you if a meeting is arranged. That way, you'll be safe no matter how the situation turns out.

in the news

When Jacob was 13 years old, he joined an adult social networking site. He met a boy online. The boy sent a picture that he claimed was of himself. He also mentioned school in his messages. The boy suggested they meet in real life, so they made a plan.

The night before the meeting, Jacob's father used Jacob's password to check his page. He was suspicious when he learned the meeting was supposed to happen in a men's toilet at the shopping centre. He called police. The next day police waited at the meeting spot. The person who showed up expecting to meet Jacob was not a young boy at all. He was a 22-year-old convicted criminal.

Jacob's name is made up to protect his privacy, but the story is true.

Ways to deal

No matter how cautious you are online, you can't always avoid trouble. Suppose someone threatens you online. Or maybe a stranger approaches you at school using information from your site. What if a friend is posting private information or meeting up with strangers?

It can be scary to find yourself in these situations. But you can take control in order to stay safe and keep having fun online.

basic safety tips

Refuse to answer cyberbullies, and block their messages.

Report any threats or inappropriate behaviour to site administrators.

Talk to a parent or trusted adult about what's happening. It's OK to tell a friend's secrets if keeping quiet might put him or her in danger.

If a stranger approaches you in real life, talking about your site, call the police.

Safety weapons

Another great way to protect yourself online is to keep your accounts private and safe. On social networking sites, you should be able to set your page to private. This action makes sure no one but your approved list of friends can read your posts and see your pictures.

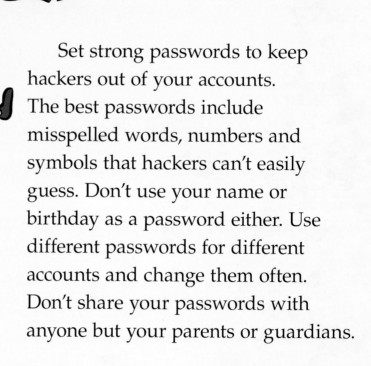

Set strong passwords to keep hackers out of your accounts. The best passwords include misspelled words, numbers and symbols that hackers can't easily guess. Don't use your name or birthday as a password either. Use different passwords for different accounts and change them often. Don't share your passwords with anyone but your parents or guardians.

You used your birthday as a password when you signed up for a social networking account. One day you get a phone call from a friend who is upset that you posted a mean message to her site. The strange thing is, you didn't write that post.

What do you do?

Online Fun

It's a bit of a downer to always talk about the things not to do on social networking sites. But there are tons of things you can do that are both safe and fun. A few ideas:

Share your creative work, such as poetry or art, with online friends.

Chat with friends you know from school or other activities. Talking with friends you already know means you don't have to worry about strangers.

Play games through networking sites with faraway relatives. It's a great way to keep in touch.

In the news

Josie had few friends. Bullies picked on her at school. But she did have one thing going for her. She was a talented writer. When she turned 16, she created a social networking page and started sharing bits of her writing. Before long she had a huge following that included most of her classmates. Through social networking, Josie gained the confidence she needed at school. She started writing for a creative writing magazine. She also worked with fellow students to write a one-act play.

Josie's name is made up to protect her privacy, but the story is true.

27

Social networking can be lots of FUN!

Summing it up

Staying safe on social networks isn't much different from staying safe in real life. You already know how to protect yourself by steering clear of strangers. You know you should keep your parents or guardians in the loop about your activities. You also know that feelings can be hurt if you blurt out mean comments about other people.

Of course, things are a little different when you're on a social networking site. It's easy to forget that someone else will read your comments and possibly pass them around. It's easy to find yourself in conversations with strangers. It's also easy to hide what you're doing from your parents.

Just remember, social networking is more than an online activity. It's a part of real life. When you're online, stick to the same rules you'd use when you're not. And you'll keep your time online useful, safe and fun.

Just stick to the rules that keep you SAFE.

Glossary

consequence result of an action

cyberbully person who uses technology to spread mean messages, rumours or threats

geotagging marking a video or photo with a location

identity who you are

loan money borrowed from a bank

pose pretend to be someone else

publication book, magazine or newspaper

reputation your worth or character, as judged by other people

restriction rule or limitation

Read more

Online Predators and Privacy (Stay Safe Online), Eric Minton (Power Kids Press, 2014)

Social Networks and Blogs (Mastering Media), Lori Hille (Raintree, 2011)

Wireless-wise Kids: Safe ways to use mobile and wireless technology, Lyn McLean (CreateSpace Independent Publishing, 2012)

Website

www.bullying.co.uk/cyberbullying/

Learn more about cyberbullying at BullyingUK.

age-appropriate sites 6
apps 14, 15

body language 10

cyberbullies 7, 11, 12, 17,
 22, 23

facial expressions 10

geotagging 12

online
 misunderstandings 11

parents or trusted adults
 20, 21, 23, 29
passwords 21, 24
photographs 12, 13, 16,
 18, 20, 21, 24
privacy settings 24
private information 8, 9,
 15, 16, 22
public information 8, 9

reputation 4, 12, 18, 19

strangers 22, 23, 29
 meeting in real life
 20, 21, 22